INTENSIFICATIONS

INTENSIFICATIONS

poems by

AUSTIN STRAUS

RED HEN PRESS | LOS ANGELES, CA

Book layout by Sydney Nichols

Cover art by Austin Straus
Author photo by Rik Pagano

ISBN: 978-1-59709-005-6
Library of Congress Card Cataloging Number: 00-105394

The Annenberg Foundation, the James Irvine Foundation, the Los Angeles
County Arts Commission, Department of Cultural Affairs, Los Angeles,
and the National Endowment for the Arts partially support Red Hen Press.

First Edition

Published by Red Hen Press
Los Angeles, CA
www.redhen.org

ACKNOWLEDGMENTS

Grateful acknowledgment is made to the editors of the following magazines and anthologies where some of these poems previously appeared: *Alternate Routes, Amorotica* (Deep River Press), *Angel's Gate Poetry Book, Antenna, The Bad Henry Review, Black Bear Review, Blue Light Review, Café Solo, California State Poetry Quarterly* (CQ), *Catalyst, Celebration, The Comic Spirit* (California State Long Beach), *Direction, Downtown News* (Los Angeles), *Electrum, Essence of Dragon Wings, Free Venice Beachhead, From Daughters and Sons to Fathers: What I've Never Said* (Story Line Press), *High Performance, The Hungry Poet's Cookbook* (Applezaba Press), *Juggler's World, The Margarine Maypole Orangutang Express, The Maverick Poets* (Gorilla Press), *Minotaur, Multiples, Negative Capability, New Letters, Nycticorax, Open 24 Hours, Ormfaer, Papeles de la Frontera, Pinchpenny, Poetic Justice, Poetry Flash, Poetry/LA, Poetry Loves Poetry* (Bill Mohr, Editor, Momentum Press), *The Reaper, The Small Pond Magazine of Literature, Snow Summits in the Sun* (Blair Allen, Editor, Cerulean Press), *Taurus, This Sporting Life* (Milkweed Editions), *Thunder Sandwich, Vol. No. Magazine,* and *Wind Magazine.* Special thanks to Wanda Coleman for her encouragement and help.

Contents

for Sascha and Ian

To The Reader

Whoever you are, here
is a note not found in a bottle
or shoved under your door or
taped to your fridge. It's from
me, a stranger, whose most sincere
desire, at this precise moment, is
to hold you close in my arms
with these words. Feel my warmth,
smell my sweat, listen closely
to my whispers. As you take in
what I say, I enter you
more intimately, more profoundly,
perhaps, than a lover, leaving,
I hope, an indelible
impression, pleasant, private,
just between us. I savor this
instant as much as you do.
Let us begin our embrace.

The Intensifier

(in memoriam Walt Whitman)

I am the Intensifier

Within each frame
the heard   the seen   the known
ignites

I am the central light

At the core
of my focused grasp
all things maximize

I tell no lies
though lies are told to me

I make all truths truer
I surprise the world with light

I sing flowers and drink moonmists

My thoughts are slow foaming sea waves
My heart the flutter of wings

I am the Intensifier
of fragments

I mix ingredients in my cauldron brain,
live each moment's miracle
with every particle of being

I am the universal animation

My blood runs wherever liquid runs

All life and form and color shape me,
make me shine

I am an energy, a spume, a flux

All things dazzle round my pivotal stand

I am the secret and the mystery and the question
answered

My answer is: Intensity
To glow, to burn
to exchange inner for outer
outer for inner, constantly, openly,
fearlessly, without shame

I am the Intensifier

No creation is alien to me

My love startles the wind
and makes the hills laugh

Each striving thing strives with my strength
and strengthens me

I am the Intensifier

The Inventor Worm

From Encyclopedia Britannica, *"Inventions and Discoveries," by E.E. Free*

it is customary
and justifiable

    for evolutionists
    to speak of

        the invention of
        the backbone

            by some species of
            primitive worm

                which developed the ability
                to stiffen itself

                    against the flowing water of
                    ancient streams

Boy in a Sailor Suit

Cute as a button, sucking
a long, thick, hard, salty
pretzel, Brooklyn, circa
1944, war still on and
just starting school.
Clever, spoiled, smart-aleck,
brat, "Guy" my middle name,
Austin Guy Straus, what a
weighty moniker for a boychik
to carry! "Austin" instead of
Abraham, my dead grandpa's
name, because the kids would have
called me "Department Store,"
after the local Abraham and Straus.
So I was "Austin," Austin for life.
"Horsechin," Lenny Umans called me.
Aunt May, who thought she knew
everything, said they'd call me
"Stinky." No one ever did, except
her, maybe. Avrum, my Hebrew name.
Austin among the Kennys, Stevies,
Seymours Alans Irvings and Joes.
Good-looking little bonditt in a
sailor suit, sucking on his pretzel,
a cocky smirk on his perfect puss,
prince of the whole damn planet.

The Coach

"Never run in glass shoes,
they might break
if you hit a rock.

Always run forward, never
backwards, so you don't
get squashed by a truck.

And be sure to pick yourself up
after you fall down
if you ever fall down . . ."

Oh coach, you were there
whenever I needed you, like
the time I scraped my arm

you drove by in your car
and yelled out as you passed,
"better get that fixed, son,
you're bleeding!"

NOTHING

there was a skinny shrimp in schoolyard days
who was known as
"Nothing"

they called him that right to his face,
he answered to it,
"Nothing"

they scrawled it on walls and fences,
in obscene jokes,
 "Nothing"

I wonder if, when he grew up,
he made Something
out of "Nothing"

ANOTHER OLD PHOTO

Bar-mitzvah day. Peach-fuzz face,
light summer suit with padded shoulders,
fat tie, and shiny, new, too-tight shoes.

We're in our backyard
after my triumphant boy-soprano rendition
of the traditional Haphtarah.

My best friend Nat, who later
twice betrayed me; my brother Dennis
to whom I never speak

flank me, pale
and smiling, companions
in malaise.

Brooklyn sunlight dwindles down
through frying Flatbush leaves.
June 12th 1952 and I know nothing,

milkily complacent,
naively numb to horror beyond
and worse to come,

unable, then, to sense
the damage, how bludgeoned my heart,
how sodden my brain.

Painful, now, to gaze
at that obscenely smooth
unworried kisser, knowing it's

mine, that innocent *punim*
still hidden somewhere under this
gray/white beard.

What would I have done
had I known? Was there anything
they could have told me
that I'd have understood
or listened to?   Of course not.
Drenched in ignorance, aglow

with the familial curse,
know-it-all to the bone, petrified
in the genes. And smiling.

THE TURNING POINT

Because my last name began with STR
me and Lenny Umans got lopped off
from Mrs. Halperin's fifth grade class
and instead of going to Mrs. Harmon's
progressive sixth grade class
where they talked sex and
everyone was competitive and smart

I wound up in purple-haired Mrs. Wilson's
class full of schnooks
where I won every spelling bee
and was the only one to make SP
after spending the whole year
figuring out ways not to get beat up
by Irving Becker or Philip MacInerny.

And that was the turning point,
the reason why I've never won
a juicy prize or kept a great job or had
moolah enough to be a nabob.

Oh I was permanently scarred
doomed to outsiderhood
surviving among nogoodniks, in terror
of my life.

And when my essay on TB
won the PTA essay contest
(after skillful editing out of my
cheap old encyclopedia)
did it dawn on me how deeply

I'd been wronged, did
I throw their indifference in their faces,
did I cry, "Tis most unfair
to condemn a child prodigy
to life among the rabble!"

No. I kept my trap shut
because by then I believed I belonged there,
that it would have been a mistake
to have dropped me in with the smarties,
that I deserved to spend my days
dodging fists and insults
showing off my spelling, cracking wise
and tricking bullies into belting other bullies
and leaving me alone.

Casualty Of War

From The Brooklyn Eagle, *May 3, 1945*

Despondent
        because he could not
        adjust himself
        to civilian life
        after his discharge
        from the American Army

                German-born Kurt Chrisgler
                43
                of 162 Linwood St
                        hanged himself
                        in his room today
                        police of the Miller Avenue Station
                        reported.

                        One end of the rope
                                from which
                                his body
                                hanged
                                had been tied
                                to the outside
                                doorknob
                                and the rope
                                had been run
                                over the transom.

The body
        was found
        by Mrs. Martha Kriesel
        a sister
        with whom Chrisgler lived.

She told police
he had been "bewildered"
by civilian life
and had been unable to find
employment.

        He was discharged
        from military service
        because he was overage
        and suffered
        from a sinus condition
                she said.

Dreaming New York

No catalogue of streets or names or neighborhoods to call you up,
    New York
always in my mind, mind wound with your streets, aglare
        with your lights, resounding with your noise, New York
you're part of me, my veins and nerves a map of you, a glow
           of you, I traffic in your flow, your blare my sunshine
           your gray rain my down, you are me big town and I am
           you, New York
faces, races, foods and moods, lonely crowds and lost alleys,
           empty IND stations two in the morning concentration camps
           asleep in metal bars and electric death
your all-night Chinatown kitchens steaming noodles and Mandarin
           clouds, your potholed cobbled cracked snow-covered or
           tarsteaming impassable never-finished streets, New York
hardened arteries varicose veins blood
        rotten teeth and cavities and pus
        your dark stinking holes, New York
reflections upon reflections upon reflections of yourself
        crazy mirrors along giant money halls Park Avenue,
        your lousy caricature of yourself, wealth, hustle
        and hustlers, sex, dogshit and gangrene beggars,
        everything together in one place, one square vibrant block
        of you, New York
You're the whore and the wino and the fool in me
you're the Jew and the hair and the scholar in me
you're the rush of words and the fast walk and the nut in me,
    New York
you're where I was born and how I was formed and who I know
    and what

I see the world through your multi-colored windows
I see the world touched with your jeweled fingers
I see the world round your fat smoking cigar stacks, New York

In my mind always, strangled with your streets and telephone lines
        sloshed in your Boweries
        smashed in your schools
        squashed in your gutters

        designed by you
        resigned to you
        unable to live without you for long,
        New York

You sing in me
my very voice a song of you
I am a New York sound
inescapably a New York voice,
for better and for worse
a New York mind

At the Table

Pass the cliché please . . .

More nostalgia? one lump
or two? Needs a bit more
ambiguity, no?

(How your pretentious
chewing of silence
rattles my digestion!)

More cliché please . . .

How's the broiled
generalization tonight?

Delicious.

Maybe a pinch more
folksy humor?

No thanks, I already . . .

Mmm, Ma, you really cooked this
contradiction to perfection.

(How does she stand
those canned
exaggerations,
pontifications
made from concentrate?)

A toast
in hackneyed liquors!

To your long and happy
soggy piecrust!

Anybody want the last
piece of cliché?

Fog, New York

tonight
I am in
volved
in a most re
vealing
fog;
un in
vited
I've in
vaded it,
wander my dogs
in its in
timate
in
veigling
embrace;
veiled in
obscurity,
I see more
clearly;
a broken bench
is as broken
as broken gets;
each branch,
stone & shadow
more than ever
itself;
a delitescent
fruity ex
humation
of afterrain

every foot and paw
fall
twig click
dry stem crunch
sharp and clean;
above, the city
clangs with
fire;
streetrees
high brick angles
& sky beyond
all
one
shell red
glow;
below,
faint
fog figures
blend with trees &
benches/as in film or
dream . . .
strangeness of
strangers is
stranger
than ever;
and always
at my approach
fog
shrinks back
like a man-shy
girl;

leaf & loam
per
fuses the atmo (s) p
here;
I am completely
at home
this fog

there remains the
startling parti c (u)
larity
of things,
& away,
far away,
the fog

First-Born

for Roz

Ma thinks I'm great,
a genius who can't do wrong, and
so what if I'm nuts,
it's part of my charm.

When I'm fired again
and tell Ma the boss
was a jerk, she commiserates, hopes
I "find something to suit my brains."

Ma still wants me to come home often,
marry a nice Jewish nonsmoking girl,
live nearby and always wear a sweater.

It's disconcerting to know
that even if I were a mass killer
caught in the act with sizzling Uzi

Ma would be there explaining to the cameras
that I couldn't possibly have done it
or that even if I did, I must have had a reason
(probably everyone murdered deserved it)

because I'm a sensitive boy
who always cleans his plate,
holds open doors, tells clever jokes
and phones his mommy daily.

A real sweet son of a
mother.

TALKING MYSELF OUT OF A DEPRESSION

Invalidations and rejections.
Shall I push through with a rash fist
or   sit
mummytight and wind
even tighter onto
now's reel
into catch and toss
flip flop
against the cold
bucket and then
food
for what?

Itching doubts smear
chilled fingers, wrists.
Breaking out in old skins
fear skin   fear skin
ticket to your collection
here a gift from the dotty keepers
come
see one infested with
word nits
who plays naked vibes
sobs silent arias   does
handstands on his own ribs

I ponder a metaphor/such
harping.
Break one
against the cliffs, color me
light, lighter, lightning

green.
On lightest green
go
tentatively
backwards
to a laughing highchair prince
or a boy kiteflying himself
over dull roofs

Or a dark natureroom
full of stuffed birds and
squirrels, teachers, pupils,
skulls, stuffed
or a schoolyard beating
kicked in the crotch
by some street tough
you don't cry
till you get home

Or when one with hair of crushed petals
turned into a witching cat
with a mouth of thorns
or the first wife's festering madness
flowering in me (for revenge she's got
the boy)
or the second one playing analyst
from her shadowed study/letters
telling me how to live

Or any of the thousand sepia
vignettes

mounted in the big hanging book
in the moonlit room
just after sound came in
and the little guys started to win
remember? The kitten died or
ran away and became yellow earth
and so too the angel fish but
especially the cute frog
who just stiffened like
Bertie's husband who
looked asleep in his easy chair

And Gram in Richmond
swallowed up by the nursing home
and even the Army shrank from your
palpitations

But you squeezed out a scholarship to
booklists and nervous
blackboards full of emphatic
nullifications
(while your balls ached
and you wanted to grab
Miss Litt's long black hair
but she was so religious
rabbis blushed)

And philosophical abstractions
collapsed in bursts
of napalm
so you caseworked slums

and clashed with fascists
while tourists gawked
and you refused to sleep/dreamt
of women lost
your photo in the papers
(hawking Vietcong flags)
and your chickenshit relatives
having heart attacks

Go back five spaces and
spin the wheel.
At the church fair
a nun smiles and hands you
the wine you've won but later
after mixing scotch with wine
you vomit for an hour

The past a map of
twisted routines
avalanches, unfinished roads,
war zones, shifting borders
unexplored swamps

A pulsating globe of ways
and words
tangled like Chinese hair

And you
drowning in the corner
of a dammed vein
because your door is jammed

and she's floating in the back seat
singing bathtub ditties
and you're still the same
fish

Horny Harry

Cellar full of
hot lights over tables, a
cactus farm, rows of
prickly phalli, hairy
fingers, balls.

Upstairs
fishtanks, guppies,
he sits for hours
watching them mate,
give birth, devour
their young.

His buxom wife
frigid. Got handjobs
from his cleaning woman
at work. Overdid it, had to
have an operation to fix
his cock.

Collects porno flicks,
one where woman fucks boxer
dog.

Harmless? Was my brother's
landlord, somebody's father,
a grandpa, even. Smiles,
says "hello" when you pass him
on the street.

ARGUMENT

quick slash
of barbed words

venom-coated
to drive them home

perfect surgery

expert, clean

something vital
mortally cut

before blood
spurts

before the burn
of pain

before you know
what's died

To the Critic

You were embarrassing to walk with.

In a broadcasting voice you remarked
about people you saw, not caring
if they heard.

You made nasty cracks about
cripples and fat people, odd couples,
ugly kids, midgets, people in wigs or toupees,
their ages or noses or pimples.

When I warned that maybe
you were hurting their feelings
you laughed, as you laughed that time
you hurled a glass at me and I bled
all over the house.

I bet some of those people also bled,
wounded by your tongue, went home
to their rooms and cried
or slashed their wrists.

That too would have made you laugh.

Our Game

Lost you then caught you then
lost you again, murdered your lovers,
murdered my lovers, ran into you
accidentally at a party in SoHo,
lost you, found you, misplaced you,
over and over, briefly glimpsed you
on TV talking about (what else?) yourself,
heard you on tape reading your work
(the machine with your tape in it
later stolen), met you over pancakes
in a Los Angeles restaurant, lost you
forgot you remembered you forgot you
again and again
                unable, ever, to blot you
                out of my dreams

SCENARIO FOR A MARRIAGE SEQUENCE AS DONE BY ORSON WELLES

A gradual increase in the angle of
      avoidance of
      your eyes
      and questions

A gradual increase in the need for
      lies
      to protect my
      ever-diminishing thread
      of self-respect

An ever-widening distance between us
      as we walked
      or slept

Your side of the king-sized bed
      seeming after a while
      to be a mile,
      no, a world
      away

An ever-thickening wall around our
      privacies
      a closing of doors
      a blocking-off of paths

A slow movement toward ceaseless hostilities

A violent clash
      to end all violent clashes

One last explosive touching—

Then
      an endless moan.

GHOST WIFE

I wanted to kill her.
I'd push her off a cliff or slug her
over the head with an oar and
drown her.

Even now, two wives later, and she
still around, I could kill her but don't
for fear I'd fail and
she'd find me.

Oh she'd smell me out
and cut me up with her nails
or chomp me with her razorblade teeth
or hack me in chunks with an axe

Or else I'd throttle her,
and she'd come back to haunt me
worse than she haunts me now.

THE SINK

is a hard white flower
with two nickel cocks
that spout cold and colder

I wonder, lying here
in this cracked room
beneath a ceiling
pregnant with roaches
between walls full
of diplomatic rats

who the guy was, fifty,
maybe a hundred years ago
sat down and flowered a sink
to sway my thoughts to . . .

graceful sink, so solid
and white, sculpted flower
clutching last light
to your glowing stem

making of this foul dump
a hushroom forest where
dresser, table, chair, rug
are trees and grass

where sink is a sacred spout
of bee and bird and blackbug wisdom,
where sink is a holiness . . .

flower of my hotel night,
goodnight!

THE FAVOR

You did me a favor
pushing me out
the window

I learned
to fly

LET HELL TAKE BACK YOUR PRIVACIES

let them stay private until you burst
with privacies too purple to carry

fatal smoke bottled in a jar, your
twisted motley poisons

thrust them down into yourself, don't
spew them my way, yoking me to you

I'm sick of your nurtured sores, self-disgust
so deep it's beyond awareness

your private, botched murder/loves, bones
hacked and irreparable, bleating
for completion in long-lost bogs of time

let those personal rats die with you, let
their cursed claws and teeth rot with you

let your secret filth leak back to earth

ACTOR

I am the star of the movie.

We're in a large bare sunlit room
of an old school building in Queens.

I've been told to knock a wineglass
off a table. Accidentally.

I don't quite get the symbolism but
do the best I can.

The girl who's directing invents
as she goes, which would be ok
if she weren't so lost.

It's all shadow and atmosphere, all
half-baked Ingmar Bergman.

Suddenly, I see her future.
She will give up filmmaking, marry,
settle on Long Island, produce
a girl and two boys. Her husband will
disappoint her, like everything else.

I'm hungry, tired and depressed,
sorry I'd said yes.

But the bare bright room's alive
with ghosts and motes of sunlight and
possibilities. And anyway
I promised.

I grit my teeth and go on following
the confused, clichéd directions.

From now on
I write my own scripts.

Scenes from an Unfinished Opera

red night expires keening lyrics from
a Broadway bomb that never came to light

the air above our building turns to thread, drops little
wormy strings on everybody's heads

upstairs someone finds several clippings from
the scrapbook of a crazy lady who used to live here

the ghost woman poet shoves a carton of journals
into the hallway where moments later they're disappeared

on the avenue a whore slugs some hapless john
with a small black hard imitation leather purse

in the gutter a midnight pigeon pecks bread crumbs
near a newly smashed bottle of Gilbey's gin

on the sidewalk an old man falls, splits his
skull, late partygoers stare, hurry by, eyes glazed

winter's a blowjob, tosses yet another bottle under
yet another bus; loaded, spring skulks just around the corner

in the tiny triangular park mid-street
a wino hums a tune, belches, farts, forgets the melody

ANOTHER DIVORCE

you want dogs? I walked all four shepherds
in the park, by day and dark
and nobody dared come near; bark?
all they had to do was walk,
the four big shepherds in the park

love? you want love? I hardly miss her;
but her dogs I walked
by day and dark, yes,
I miss the dogs, the four
big shepherds in the park

Even Paranoids . . .

(in memoriam Delmore Schwartz)

Shadowed by shadows, stared at
by strangers. Silence on the phone
definitely not God's.
CIA? FBI? IRS?
Some crazed ex-girlfriend
obsessed with my number?
Eyes in the wallpaper, ears
among blossoms. Ex-wives gossip
in their memoirs, peddle diaries
for bucks. Babbled about on
talk shows/giggles and smirks.
Former lovers fire darts at my
photos. I'm the villain in nightmares,
my son's hairy monster.
Even the ocean keeps shushing
my name. Late at night, far away,
the insistent yowling of cats.
That which I'd rather keep secret
found lipsticked in toilets, scrawled
across skies. Crows mock my
excuses, curs mimic my lies.
I'm riddled by missiles shot by
unerring tongues. Mind Swiss-cheesy
with holes, brain leaking self-esteem.
An inner homunculus screeches curses
at this so-mangled existence. I turn
from the face that uglies at me
when I shave. Who's driving this
hearse, stealing my lines, rasping
through my lips words I don't

recognize? Can I trust my next move
or anything I say? What the fuck
am I up to? I'm the wrong one to ask.

Even I'm out to get me.

THINGS BREAKING

Shift of pot and dish
chips the brown cup
white

Sidewalks heave and split in rain/
root and river, nerve;
fine blades of lightning
crack the streets

Wrecked men sprawl in wine-splotched
rags; from chafed lips hang
torn tongues

Skin tracks with frown and smoke
and age

Minds like spidered glass

Walls
where New York rats
scratch through cracks
to catch a breath of park

Broken limbs stuck in mud
like butchered nudes

Cracked schemes, cracked dreams,
cracked dawns

An official's whim
cracks a citizen's life

A gunshot cracks the headlines

A lightly spoken lie
                    cracks our love

Ending

for Patrocinia

I was there, January First, 1978
gulped New York icy air
chugged down streets snorting steam
squeezed damp skies like rags
in my furious fists

You were there, burning
to the tips of your tapered fingers
difficult Panamanian
with your "I refuse" eyebrows,
your cat nares flaring a black
that matched your eyes

And we gave birth to the New Year
in your veiled parlor
defying superstition and the gods
all odds against our resurrection/
accusation and denial
stifling reconciliation

Every opening in me sucked at your
essence, wishing you were the woman sent
to test the marrow of my meaning

As January whitened outside our windows;
trees sizzled with frost, bare limbs
slowly drew on their glary, furry gloves

You sat, feet tucked under
in your panther corner,
diamond-eyed, dusky, hot,
dark-haired, distant

And I knew, as you wrapped
your soundless hurt around my heart
that our love was as dead
as the old year's corpse
and that there'd better be a quick burial
before the last fleeting sweetness of
this thing we had, this eternal, miserable,
familiar, absurd, inevitable moment

began to stink

RETURNED MAIL

Last week
I wrote you three letters,
sent a dozen poems, seven
written especially for you.

This week, from you I got
one letter, containing two pages,
Xeroxed copies of our annulment.

Thanks for answering.

TORN

threefold remembrance:
the crossed path, the first kiss,
the curse of caring

imbedded terrors, the way time
curls in clusters like wallpaper
peeled by fingernails

the hills roll past the
speeding car, the sea rolls up,
a sparkling carpet, then

lies still, brooding; the moon
at dawn, pale as
a cat's eye at noon

my life turned upsidedown,
an hourglass, all my days return
their bits of beauty

I hold your face
close in my hands, taste cold lips,
nibble you into oblivion . . .

THIS POEM WOULD RATHER NOT HAVE A TITLE

suddenly everything strikes me as odd, the construction
of my finger or the way this room is put together

suddenly not a thing seems definitely as it ought to be,
preordained and certain, the necessary result of some prior cause

why must chairs look like *this*, I wonder
and the human face take this particular form?

and isn't it quite boring that mighty oaks from tiny
acorns grow, that all seeds of things become those very things

the obsessive regularity of nature, of day and night, birth and
death and seasons, the unreasonable sameness of it

I find appalling, galling, chilling, dulling, deadly;
suddenly I wish everything were different

give chairs wings, for instance, and call them bears
and let bears glow green and speak in tongues, I mean

everything seems awfully wrong, the wrong people in the
wrong jobs, the wrong streets lined with the wrong houses

and trees all the wrong colors! and the shapes that people take,
the ugly noises they emit! I'd rather they spoke

music, harps and bassoons, piccolos and cornets, and I'd like
some purple people, some blue, some striped, some dotted

and their hair, Jesus, their hair would be made
of silk or potatoes or anything other than that tangly stuff

and why do people have hair at all, what a mess,
why not little flowers that bloom and fall?

I'm fed up with beds and walls, windows and lampposts, cars
and sidewalks, rooftops and billboards, radios and noodles

I want a cool sun and dry water and previously unknown colors
and people who love in unheard-of ways!

suddenly mere travel isn't enough,
bike riding, dart throwing, dreaming,

surrealism, madness or philosophizing,
even poetry isn't enough! I want

too much, I want to be you, or a bird, air,
or the street remembering, or a dead fish,

I want to be my own brain
writhing in its wash of memories

I want to be anything but this room
and this summer and this dumb, limited, predictable

old skin.

Austin's Book of Lists (Partial Contents)

78 women I never should have dated
93 people I never should have confided in
66 jobs I never should have taken
211 forms I never should have filled out
653 forms I was supposed to fill out but didn't
327 bills I forgot to pay
1,137 things I never should have said, not including:
47 things I never should have volunteered for and
62 things I never should have said twice

9 bits of acrobatics I never should have attempted

12 cities I'm sorry I visited
18 hotels I'm sorry I stayed in
284 restaurants I'm sorry I ate in
97 dishes I'll never order again

185 TV series I wasted time watching
119 teachers I learned nothing from
105 relatives I hope never to see again

1 ½ famous people I've known intimately
4 pets I regretted petting
19 favorite experiences of being fired
11, 827 embarrassing moments

483 books not read past the first page
110 classics I've always meant to read
74 ¼ classics I don't get why they're called classics

22 movies walked out on
59 movies I still don't know why I sat through
35 scenes in movies that made me sick
203 movie scenes I wish I were in

108 dullest topics of conversation
43 ways of killing time on a boring job
75 professions I might have succeeded in if
89 excuses for not getting out of bed in the morning
743 excuses for not looking for a job
846 reasons why I am not rich

3 people I knew who killed themselves
16 people I know who ought to kill themselves

23 New Year's resolutions I always break
109 New Year's resolutions I no longer make

28 games I no longer play
11 games I wish I could afford to play

15 musical instruments I gave up trying to play
4 musical instruments those around me wish I knew how to play

31 ice-cream flavors I have no desire to sample
37 exotic supermarket items I don't like the looks of

25 simple words I never remember how to spell
7 frequently called phone numbers I always have to look up

113 poets whose work invariably puts me to sleep
1,426 rock groups who cause me headache
2, 637 political clichés that hurt my stomach
961 idiotic obsessions
529 unshakable beliefs, opinions and prejudices
124 lifelong self-delusions

101 reasons not to start a list of lists

THE JUGGLER

The only juggler in history able
to juggle 10 balls or 8 plates
was the Italian, Enrico Rastelli . . .
born in Samara, Russia, on December 19,
1896, and died in Bergamo, Italy,
on December 13, 1931.
—The Guinness Book of World Records

Died
at thirty-five, not even.

Did juggling
do him in?

Maybe that eleventh ball
or ninth plate

he just couldn't orbit
with the others

or the tension of sustaining
ten or eight

night after night
show after show

broke his heart
like a dish.

The Heart-Shaped Room

Divorced and staying with my parents
I am, in a way, home
but my dreams are nightmares
and I'm obsessed with my son.

I try to focus on something,
a green, diamond-shaped dresser knob
or an oval mirror
or one of the framed photos of me
at various stages in my career
as a child.

Why I've come here, obscure;
why I stay, unclear. The lure of California,
the weather, beaches, women, friends,
or just to rest or escape from
what I must do; reasons enough.

Yet I could go crazy in such a room
as I have in such a room before.

Maybe I'll leave sooner than planned.

Changing plans is becoming
my big frisson, as if
to make, then break,
is a higher, more intense form
of choosing.

I've been accused of acting
on whims, as if this were
a character flaw.

I say, have the courage of
your whims.

But their terrible hesitancy
weakens my bones.

In a room of my parents' house
a man wakes in the dark
surprised to find himself
a child.

THE OLDEST KID IN CLASS

He refuses promotion; still
doesn't get logarithms or fractions,
gerunds or Greek.

Don't graduate me. Don't kid me.
Teach me something. What's it
about? What's that life
out there, those stunned
expressions, the way everything lovely
seems to get ruined. Give me
some tools. What must I know?
Crooks and fakers? Landlords? Cops?
Speechwriters? Racists? The tactics of
lawyers and agents, the nature of love?
Answer me some basics, like how to
make money doing something great.
I don't care if there's homework.

Nightscape

Moon
red to white to red
filling and unfilling, wine
in a cracked glass globe . . .

A squat bush perched on canal rocks
green or aquamarine by day,
blueblack at night, gulps
stray children.

Distant houses. A window excited
by darkness, blinking,
beating time
to the pulsing stars . . .

A sea-stirring. Green foam, circles
of yellow-gray moonlight; a thin stalk,
barely visible, risen above the surface,
a glowing emerald eye . . .

Little puffy rushings
of sand or dry grass
somersault across lawns,
boneless acrobats . . .

Wind's fuzzy whisperings . . .
Night enters my eyes, I
inhale its music, darken
into one of its creatures, become

whatever it wants . . .

WE WERE SO HIGH

we didn't walk
on the water

we walked
on the *sheen*
on the water

At the Concert in La Jolla

The audience is white, all white, and so is the music
    and the musicians and the walls
    of the museum where hang the latest works
    of the avant garde, giant sterilities
    proceeding on the assumption that
    a blown-up sterility is somehow more
    valuable than a tiny sterility, on
    analogy, perhaps, with the size of lies...

And the music, Beethoven, Janacek, Schubert, exactly
    as if recorded, slick, too slick,
    I nearly dozed, beautiful music no doubt
    but something missing in the music,
    in the four flawless performers in their formal
    dress, in the perfectly attentive high-toned
    audience, in the scientifically correct
    air-conditioned atmosphere...

The answer I found in the same museum in glass cases
    where, neatly arranged, and despite their labels
    indicating that they were, each and every one,
    stolen from some other culture, sat the ancient
    brown pre-Columbian figurines with the broad
    Indian cheekbones

Listening during the concert to the classic strains,
    the intermission chitchat, the conquering race
    at rest, absorbing *Kultur*, listening
    with a bitter smile on each clay face...

Is There A Poem?

buried in my eyes
or under the rug or in the faucet's slow
slow drip or maybe where the cockroach sleeps?

where does the poem crouch before it
fleeks out of darkness
on sparkling melodious stallions?

is that a poem squeezed between
silences at 3 a.m. while faucets
drum/tap and the cockroach skrits?

and as I'm sirened into dream
does the poem begin to fuse,
a little glowing tuft

floating towards me
bearing its cargo of
unknown, yet oddly familiar,

gifts?

Recreation Day

On recreation day
hordes of flabby Americans
squeeze out of houses
onto lawns
or into cars to get to lawns
to play games and drop fat
in the grass, all so

furiously recreating
that the very heavens vibrate
with their squeals and
arguments, shouts of "FORE!"
and "LOVE-THIRTY!"
and "STRIKE TWO!"

bouncing off all the high peaks
of the Andes, Alps and
Himalayas,
so sweatful and juicy and
puffy with smells of steak and pork

that all the poor and hungry
of the world come running
to lick the air
as it settles
full of molecules of
rich American flesh

Moonlight Walk

I went out into midnight
to cool my blood

and found October
making moonlight love.

There are old men's wrinkles
in gnarled trees.

There are sounds one hears
only among flickering shadows.

No matter how slowly I passed
I seemed to walk too fast.

I thought I heard a bird
dreaming.

DIVORCE NOISES

You're an acid accusation eating into me from afar.

You try with some success to shred my heart in that
      grating machine
      your voice.

On the telephone you must make your tone
      do all the work, the work of eyes and gesture
      and frown,
      show disdain, dismissal and contempt.

I see you through those sounds.

Your sharp little teeth, your oh so soft when
      they want to he lips
      curled now in a sneer

Your dark eyes narrowed, catty, flashing
      in the tainted gloom.

And, after I, like a much-wounded soldier,
      have parried your thrusts
      with my shield of rage

Did I detect in your voice a hint of the old softness?

Or was I only yearning to hear you, hold you, have you,
      soft?

The Day I Killed My Conscience

No sleep all night, knowing
what I had to do.

It was sick, beyond help, terminal,
in terrible pain.

Poor thing whimpering, had to plug
my ears.

Avoided looking at it as I led it
to the yard.

No time for sentiment. Yes,
we'd been close for years.
Yes, I'd miss it. But
I had to be tough.

Wanted to end it fast
but it stared at me so hard I had to
blindfold it.

Aimed the gun, foresaw a mess.

Tied the whole thing in a bag and drove out
to the pier, threw it off
and watched it sink.

Ha! I feel a hundred pounds lighter
and ready for anything.
Able to cheat, lie, torture, slaughter,
murder for hire. Do the nine to five.
A man without qualms. Dangerous.

VIEW FROM 4ᵗʰ AND BROADWAY

Raining. Bus stop. Strangers. Waiting
for something to pick me up, a bus,
sunshine, found money, a drink or smoke,
a passing girl who smiles.

West on Broadway above the Pacific
there's a bright blue streak
for the sun to slide down
to where it hangs out nights.

What bedraggled travelers!
Even the young seem bent, cursed,
crushed, blind to everything
but self-projected pain.

And here I am,
gazing up beyond rain, sky, time, thinking
maybe I'll never reach the end of the line
if I keep on switching buses.

Raining. Bus stop. Strangers. I wait
for something to pick me up, a bus . . .

CHAUVINIST

no gang ever came to drag away your father
  bring him back
  broken, unable to sit or sleep
  every section of his body
  beaten raw

no, no one ever did that to your father

and they never actually held you down and
kicked you, spit and pissed on you, insulted you
electroshocked you

no they never did that

so you persist in thinking kindly of them
saying they're "basically decent men doing a tough job
keeping your best interests uppermost"

yeah

so you survive in your comfortable narrow corners
pursue your comfortable narrow pleasures with
your comfortable narrow mates

since they've never taken away your father
or held you down and hurt you
and your only nightmares come from heartburn,
money troubles, aging, boredom, stress

because the hurts they've given
have entered you secretly,
converted you to complicity and
cowardice, made you
one of them

FASHIONISM

trim the treetops   color all walls gray
dancing in the streets banned
or dancing with one eye closed
no grass where sidewalks grow
straight lines everywhere
queue up   line up   all heads shorn
or shaven

shave the poets   shave the crazies
shave the soldiers   helmets must
                    fit snugly
starched uniforms   starched muscles

this week's color: beige
with black stripes

shine black boots and shoes
all metal gleams

we will have no recalcitrant sunsets

all conversations to start with
"Hail the Mighty Fist of Fashion!"

no spitting near government bookstores

music banned except for beige music
with black stripes

all adornments on uniforms banned
everybody must wear a uniform

no buttons with slogans or pictures

the color red and several shades of
yellow and green are banned

all barracks must fly the flag of fashion

no coughing sneezing tittering or
inattention during readings from the masters

violators will be hung upside down
and beaten at intersections

no living outside government-regulated
compounds

no traveling except by pass and in
official vehicles

liquor narcotics stimulants beer coffee
curried and spiced foods
strictly forbidden

mumbling frothing gargling loud chewing
slurping dirty noses fatness laziness
nausea depression sleeping late lateness
wobbling limping blinking staring at the moon
hesitating farting pissing outside government
toilets public displays of affection between
sexes or between humans and animals picking
flowers breathing too deeply aimless walking

reading proscribed texts   reading upside down
singing alone   marching backwards   making faces
defacing government signs   writing on walls or
sidewalks   writing secretly or keeping a diary
printing without official seal   writing backwards
or in cipher   using an unofficial language or word
refusal to bow, kneel or kowtow to officials
substituting obscene words in official songs or
documents

all punishable offenses

theft of government property   mimicking
of officials   laughter at solemn ceremonies
sabotage or cackling

capital offenses

shred the garbage   burn the dissidents' books
isolate the rebels

anyone who mutilates, befouls
or ridicules the flag of fashion
shall be publicly tortured

hard work   incentives for those
who most closely resemble
a machine

rewards for those who exceed quotas
payoffs for informers

scapegoat of the month: people with turned-up
noses

jokes forbidden
female children forbidden
houseplants forbidden

sighing moaning complaining throwing rocks
or other missiles
forbidden

it is recommended by the high committee
for fashionable acts
that all citizens repeat at least twenty times
a day
passages from the works of the masters
loudly
and especially for the edification
of children and women

no sex for the unproductive
no sex between cats

the ant shall be the official insect of the month
every month

destroy all lovers of wind
sybarites shall be tortured

he who endeavors to remember anything
but official wisdom
shall be lobotomized

trim the treetops   color all walls gray
dancing in the streets banned
or dancing with one eye closed
no grass where sidewalks grow

death to criminals and deviants

Long live the Kingdom of Fashion!

On Viewing Photos of Dead Nicaraguan Children

these children seem to be playing
the way children play at sleep

covered with dirt, just
children, playing

but this one's face is gone
and that one's arm

and no sleeping child ever had
that one's wide-eyed stare

dead children, yes, murdered children
the look and stench

and they are, were, children
and I still can't comprehend

why

No Cure for This Life

Even frivolity has its place. Absurd
hobbies, silly customs, the existence of
The Queen. Let them have pie-eating
contests, situation comedy and quiz shows.
I mourn the possible loss in nuclear
catastrophe of masterpieces as well as
pizza, poodles and funny hats.

Let schlock live along with
Shakespeare. Let it all thrive, even
Harlequin Romances, cockroaches and
crocodiles, crabgrass and posies, frisbees,
French fries and fatty burgers.

If only bombs destroyed disease
and hunger, injustice, ignorance.
No chance. If only this magnificent mess
survived its leaders. Stayed lovably
ridiculous. Stayed what it is.

Just stayed.

THE MACHINATORS

I know a sculptor who puts dolls in machines
and when a pin's released there's a sudden spin
and zap! the doll's decapitated.

There's an artist somewhere who builds
twisty aquariums he fills with fish
then throws a switch that fries them.

Of course these characters are only mildly
dangerous, compared to some. At least their
damage is limited to fish and dolls.

But look out!
You may be right now
snoozing in a chair

that's going for
a little ride
or floating in someone's aquarium

and whoever's pulling the pin
or throwing the switch
is no artist

so the job
is bound to be
botched.

THIRTEEN MORE WAYS OF LOOKING AT A BLACKBIRD

1.

Ruined land.
Mud and scarred trees.
A blackbird paces
a high dry stone.

2.

In this photo, a shadow
across your face.
The blackbird's wing?

3.

A blank canvas.
The blackbird's just left or
is about to arrive.

4.

A blackbird passes.
We must be thinking of one another.

5.

An unintelligible whispering.
The sea, the moonlight, and
the blackbird.

6.

Pigeons are often found smashed
in the road. Never
a blackbird.

7.

Planted field glimpsed
from speeding train. A single
blackbird
punctuates the monotone.

8.

In a bright cool room
the pragmatic lamps
cry for a blackbird.

9.

Above my head the wind
plays delicate percussives.
Somewhere, a blackbird listens.

10.

It rains and rains
and will never stop raining.
A blackbird pecks my brain.

11.

Fallen asleep
In the belly of the blackbird.

12.

From out a corner of a dream,
blackbirds, drawing after them
the drapes of evening.

13.

Some things I cannot hold:
fire, disappointment,
the blackbird flying.

AFTER THE RAIN

The trees are feeding
green
green suck
green root
wet tongue tangle
lapping the sunken
earth
green lip
slurp
of sumptuous
mud

The trees are eating
green
green urge
green blood
upsurging lust
of green, green

and if I stand here
long
I too will root
and sprout
and heave a shout
of green

SUPERSTITIONS

Avoid sidewalk-painted circles.
White cats. Wild dogs. Ladders.
Mean-faced strangers.

Left shoe on first. Don't say
 "accident" while driving.

Squash no spiders, ants
or anything that moves (except
roaches and flies).

Steer clear of unlit streets.
Stop to sniff roses. Smile
at passing children.

Exert extra care on Mondays.
Carry a toy camel, scout knife,
seven emergency dollars and
seven photos of your woman.

The third wife
is the keeper.

Be a cat. Use every life
you've got.

THE JOB

It lurks out there,
smelly, toothsome, hairy, slinky,
and I wait, sans loincloth, spear,
sweaty in collar, jacket, tie, pinched shoes,
poised to pounce when The Job, in its ficklehood,
deigns to emerge from whatever
asphalt or brick or file cabinet cave
it squirms in while scheming its devious
ways. The Job is a tease and a monster,
and, till captured, a myth, cousin of unicorn,
griffin, chimerical many-headed, slippery
beast. I wait, sharpening glances,
holding breath, ready to sliver that sucker
when I spot it.

The Job. Damn thing! I smell it.
The Job I don't want. The Job
I'd rather not have. The Job
I must hunt. The Job out there.

One of us will be devoured.

KILLING WEEDS

my boss hands me the shears, says
"clip the weeds, they're ugly"

me, I like anything wild, green
struggling to live between cracks
under a hot sun

but I do my job like a good
soldier, clip the weeds, even begin
to enjoy the carnage

"take that you little bastards!"
"gotcha, you dirty weed!"

I'm careful, however, not to destroy
roots, know that
while me and the boss
and the others
keep looking for things to kill

weeds come back on dark nights
thinking weed thoughts
smiling weed smiles

THE DOUBLE

Linda Bergen's twin
with the same bitten nails
lank brown hair
and slim small-breasted
body, the pouting
mouth, pale sickly
skin, chain-smoker's
wrinkles, terrible
posture and little-girl
helpless expression

gets on the Wilshire bus

and I say, "Linda, it's
you, whatta you doing
in L.A.?"

and she turns and says,
"I'm Doris, not Linda,
but what are YOU doing
in L.A., Michael?"

and I'm not Michael.

EVIDENCE

I return to my apartment to find
a spear right through
the refrigerator.

I sigh and frown.
Stink of home: sweat-
beaded ceilings, plans
rotting, dreams gone moldy.

The strangled calendar, barely
breathing, croaks,
"June, it's June."

The lonely plant, pale and fading,
pleads for water.
I sprinkle it off the critical list.

Chunks of air crouch in corners
like petrified cats.

On being opened, windows
sneer and screech.

Murdered books everywhere, pages
poked up stiffly.
One recent novel hoarsely mutters,
"Read me, read me."

Rug, bed, tables, kitchen,
all unsolved cases.

The moldy bathroom glowers, its
privacy invaded. The shower is rusty.
I note the vegetation
clinging to the tiles,
faint growls and coughing.

A smelly sock moans to be
thrown in with the laundry.
I sink a jump shot.

Severed tongues of manuscripts
loll out of cartons. Paintings,
gone crazy glaring at each other,
bleed down walls.

Someone used to live here.

Playing Daddy

Me tossing a plastic ball and Ian
slugging it and passersby
applauding.

I recall my father
equating fatherhood with baseball,
football, handball and
showing off.

Swing that bat, baby, c'mon and kill it,
knock it over my head!

This is the soft part of playing papa,
the fun part, without tears.

Choke up on the bat, kid, now kill it!
Whatta slugger!

The tough part's later, requires
sacrifice, guts and selfless giving.
The tough part's not worrying about payback,
except maybe a smile.

C'mon and kill it kiddo!
But know this: I love you
even if you miss the ball.

THE LEAF

I nailed a big green leaf to my white bedroom wall
and now it's a wrinkled umber ball
rolled up not into a question but
a nameless gall all its own

a shell or an ear, a convoluted
turned-in-upon-itself brain; brown bat
wrapped in browner wings or
parched hills, ridged with pain.

It hangs, empty and dry, a skin
from which green dreams have flown,
a skin I've writhed in, thrown off, my
ever-shedding mind.

It hangs, a crimped cup
holding nothing but its own echoing shadows,
dying past death into
a particular perfection

closing as imperceptibly
and gently as an arthritic fist,
crushing its inner
darknesses

into an idea
too complex, delicate
and amazing
to be known.

TEMPTATIONS

Tempted to turn thistle,
let breezes blow me to bits.
I've a crazy wish to be frizzed
by dragon breath
or sail wingless off a cliff
into the sea's jagged teeth.

Tempted by rain to stand still
for eons, until I'm either
a smooth stone or a wide lagoon.
I must hold myself back from fiddling
with sunshine or stuffing moonlight
in my underwear.

Tempted by red flowers to become red flowers,
to feel my redness flower,
to smell myself red.

Tempted to sleep with clouds
as purple sleeps; to reach a eucalyptus finger up
to catch a comet's ring; to
ask questions of the fish: how does it feel
to hear with skin?

Tempted by a potato bug
strolling a labyrinth of rose
or a potato budding in a hundred eyes
and I could be an avocado ripening to my shell
pregnant soft and oval bellied.

I long to be a rough stucco wall
zigzagging a hill, tickled by ivy,
or a long-maned black stallion with arched neck
stretching for sweet grass, big teeth
munching grass for hours,
brain thoughtless and green.

Tempted to ride with gods who shuffle tides,
run the day and night machine, whisper
their weathered and mysterious codes
into the feathery veins of numberless
susceptible flocks.

From My Office Window

An American flag sinks slowly
into Los Angeles rooftops.

Dry palmtree heads scrape
like squashed beetles.

The mountains didn't show up for work
and the sky is blue saliva.

The sunset-smeared street is a movie set
for surreal murder. I expect anything . . .

a twenty-foot crow pecking through
windows, decapitating secretaries,

a huge tank crushing cars and
pedestrians to music by Sousa,

the slow dissolution of buildings
into irregular pyramids of sand.

I am peering out of a bathysphere
lowered from another life. I am

not really here, not really (repeat
endlessly, wear out reality) here . . .

Ad in a New Zealand Newspaper

lost
in Birnham Wood
bald
one-eyed
ginger tom cat
crippled in both back legs
neutered

answers to the name of
Lucky

If I Were a Wall

there'd be obscenities,
political slogans
and initials of dead lovers
scrawled in red and yellow,
blue, green and black
along my belly

and I'd hold birds of
paradise and ravens and
sparrows and all the wrens
and robins of the universe
and they'd sing and feed
and build nests and paint poems
down my sides with their shit

if I were a wall

and if I were a wall
I'd hold back the floods
and keep out the stampeding
cattle but allow every
horse to jump me and I'd
amble slowly among
houses and let my
stones mumble hymns
while the farmers slept

if I were a wall

and if I were a wall
I'd be hard and winding

as a frozen river
or soft and deadly
as a sleeping cobra
or in my meanderings
I'd be a story
written in sibilants
and curliques

if I were a wall

and if I were a wall
I'd let myself tumble into fragments
to be dug up and buried in museums
or be carved into faces that are
worshipped at midnight by
moondriven witches

if I were a wall

and I'd refuse the weight
of corpses or the smack
of noon sun or gouging
by bullets or wailing of
mourners or anything but
warm drizzles and tall grass
brushing my thighs

if I were a wall

and I'd dream of entering myself
and becoming a suite of rooms
multiplying and dividing,
turning and turning
until I was an infinite cavern
all chiaroscuro and texture
where unfettered dreams
could wander in search of
unsuspecting dreamers

if I were a wall

THE GARDENERS

one poured champagne
on the rosebuds
so blossoms would
pop like bubbles

another sang ditties
to the mums
hoping they'd sing back
in a chorus of petals

the third draped his houseplants
in newspapers
wanting flowers to
burst through the headlines

and the last chewed seeds
waited for brilliant multi-
colored notions to bouquet
his brain

Poems Yet To Be Written

The poem of palpitations and tongues
the reek of love, festoons of fingertips
each petal a word newly sprung

The poem with so many sides it rolls,
a moon through mists, eyes
through orchards of incense and women

The poem seething with centuries
of pain, aching with facts and quotes
clippings and stats

The poem of the mensch, of unspoken
decencies, of soft approaches and
gut connections

The poem that is not a poem but a tree
The poem that is more caress than poem
The poem that kisses

The poem that swallows itself like a snake
The poem that refuses to stop singing
The poem that knows when to stop singing

The poem that changes profiteers into givers
and politicians into holy men, gurus
into lovers and fanatics into cats

The 800-page multi-volume opus, words
linked end to end, rising above the smog
to the moon and back

The poem of disappointing friends
The poem of a moment in a dark room
forty years ago, the poem of your juices . . .

PARTYING

I met Sam and Gertie
remarried after divorce
and miserable again

Octavia the former child
who's finally decided to
grow up (she's fifty-six)

Len and Kate
(met on a blind date)
Phyllis from Boston
Harold the dentist
Harold the lawyer
Harold the insurance man

Gabrielle who speaks no English
Fred who speaks no French
Ulan who doesn't seem to speak anything

Alice and Steve, Alice and Henry
Henry and Steve, Alice's mother Greta
Greta's mother Louise, Louise's brother
Lewis, Lewis' friend Sylvia, Sylvia's dog
Curmudgeon, Curmudgeon's friend Walter
Walter's analyst who mumbled his name
or an obscenity

Larry the agent and Larry the gangster
who turn out to be the same guy

Marty whose book just came out
Irv whose book will never come out

Eve the actress
who just finished doing a play by Mike
who is writing a new play for Diane
who isn't here because she's having
an accident with Harvey

Eve's sister the aspiring personality
Loretta
who works as a go-go dancer
and who kisses me ardently,
mistaking me for a film producer

Lorenzo the poet
who recites four lines of rhymed verse
then faints with pleasure

Burton
who catches Lorenzo for a living

Zeena the exotic dancer
Zeena's husband Al who owns a deli
their charming children Salami, Baloney,
Pastrami and little Knockwurst or
Jason or Scott or something

Daisy and Mel
the vegetarian-meditation podiatrists

Harriet and Jack and Kenny
and Dave and Marge
who live together in a Jacuzzi

April
who gives me her phone number
and urges me to call her
before she gets home

Ron the laidback Rolfer
who refuses to shake hands for free

Gladys the mime
who appears to be imitating herself

Manny and Denise
who are into dying

Herman
who once met Gurdjieff in Pasadena

Stewart and Yolande
who are at every party I ever go to

Perry and Mitzi
who fill a space beautifully

Evelyn and Jane who are
identical schizophrenics

Jamal
the songwriter/poet/actor/singer/ dancer/
filmmaker/gourmet chef/astrologer
who glowers

Barb who raves about the creativity
of Rick's latest Tampax commercial

nineteen people
with their mouths full
of wine and zucchini

numerous clever yawning children

and an octopus in a Hawaiian shirt
who does something with mergers
and blows cigar smoke in nine directions
simultaneously

THE PHILOSOPHY TEACHER

Twenty-seven, looks forty. Thinning
hair, dark-pouched eyes. Low pay,
community college, money trouble,
bus to work. New to Cal, from
Nebraska, out of sync, homesick,
miserable. Thirty-eight registered,
down to seventeen and dwindling.
He lectures, students nod, yawn,
doodle; someone always falls asleep
and snores. No one asks a question.
Talking to himself? Unreal. Scary.
First time he's taught anything.
Few pass his tests, most get D or F.
Chose the wrong profession?
Returns home drained, head
aching, vision fuzzed, craving
drink. Wife's cheery "hi" and
familiar face no help, seems
a stranger, confuses her with
a girl in class. Baby cries and cries.
Urge to strangle it squelched. Retires
early, sleepless, fidgety, hopes
to waken somewhere else. Dreams
of turning PhD into a book. Subject:
suicide, its philosophical
implications. A way to stay alive.

METAPHRASTES

(in memoriam, Bill Pillin)

I died that L.A. instant
when sidewalks made more sense
than dreams, when broken bottles and
turds, rocks and cracks spoke
more eloquently, more honestly than I
ever could

I died, and seagulls swam
in slow circles like ashes
stirred in a translucent bowl,
palm trees hung from clouds like
tassels announcing the death of lies
and I vowed on the sacred breath of
a passing cur

to rise again like a god
from this miserable curb, rise
into myself as if on film, to
traffic horns and flutes, to
the fine weavings of air that float
like shredded flags, hiding the sun,
to the fantastic lamentations
of crows

Sadist

MacArthur Park pigeons
pecking crumbs and seeds

I circle to avoid
the feeding congregation

Comes along a mean-eyed youth
who's marked my circumambulation

I sense what's next
suspect him capable of worse

Up go his arms, scattering
the frightened birds
who rise and fall
like dust

Pitiful exercise! Terror
of the drifting mind
faced with blatant peace

A chance to hurt the helpless
helplessly seized

The weakness of the weak
for power

Over Her

1940 Duke on the radio working on my headache
sirens and typewriter buzzings, faucet drippings and jazz
in bad light I write poems, my life turns corners, I
squint to catch a glimpse of where I'm going

Ellington radio headache going gone sirens buzzing dripping
jazz ripples into corners bad light poems squint I'm

over her over her over her (it says) I'm over over

Ben Webster's horn hey jazzman play that thing I'm
alone chilled hungry broke again it doesn't matter
jazzwarmed   jazznourished   painting and poming, in love
new love   and I'm
over over over over   her

play that thing . . . ooh!   over her

FOR MR. GRAPES

No cryptic remarks, tricky
techniques or academic
glitz. I talk straight,
no frills. Emotions
not sorted into piles
or secreted behind learnedly
graffitied walls, not packaged
in little pills and fed
discreetly to the elect.
I'm up front or I'm nothing.
Kid myself here and I'm phony.
I don't talk crap.

Sitting naked in the
old armchair
that stinks of me,
a second body, oozy
and reeking in
all its depths,
I itch, twist, burst
beneath my fat, ribbed
by flaws, yearning like hell
to love, be loved, redress pain,
shine, shine so hard
the world shines, stop
the ancient, gnawing, bonedeep
guilt.

I'm lucky if the next call
is not from some woman

I drove mad or a child
I ought to know better.

I'm lucky if there's a fresh can
of beer in the fridge.

Message From A Hungry Poet

I am not Gregor Samsa. Therefore
I do not understand why I have become
a giant insect.

Lying here on my hack, waving my tiny legs
(there must be three hundred of them)
crying out for help, I suddenly recall that,
unlike Gregor, I live alone. No one will come.
Not even Kafka.

After I scribble this note I will sail it
out an open window as a paper plane.
Perhaps you who've found it will bruit it
about and someone will come to help.

I have an unbearable urge to nibble
lettuce leaves. Send some, immediately,
in large denominations.

At a Pizza Parlor in Reseda

Over onions and anchovies
loud conversations after work,
the intimate affairs

I hear more than I want
about some guy's two marriages,
his companion's three-year engagement,
they seem quite friendly,
getting acquainted

The pizza's hot and fresh, the beer
slides down cool and tart, it's
a perfect snack as I avoid
the freeway traffic crush

The girl's open, liking him but hoping
he won't come on too strong, spoil
their newly budding thing

But he pushes, takes her warmth
for weakness, his wine talks, he
makes a clumsy pass which she deftly
deflects, slightly disappointed
but too decent to say so

They keep chatting, but
something's dead, I can
taste it, I've been there,
made such moves, murdered
such moments

THE PROCESS (1)

Does the dazzle of a lavish sun conceal?
Am I merely lulled by glare,
the rococo serenity of things?
Is it all a trick? Am I victimized again
by easy love?

Or, shadowminded, churlish, stupidly splenetic,
do my contracted pupils
fail to hold light,
spreading, instead, a smear of gloom
across these perfect afternoons?

What if my grizzled moods change everything:
leaf, weed, stalk of grass,
petal golden-edged, distinct, all
real only as I
relate to each?

Would that matter? If my feeling eye
makes truth, would the world wobble,
mountains shake, anything move?
I think not, yet the thought stuns:
that it all depends on me, what I am, how

I see; enough to awe my sight to blindness?
Or else force me to take more solemnly
these obligations of my senses: to dare
stench and burn and sting; the moon man,
sea changer, lightning rod.

POET POT PIE

take 18 thin pale dry-voiced poets
with words of straw

chop fine

add eleven fatty dribbling hippy-type
women who shout a lot

steam for an hour

toss in a pinch of drunken lipsticky
wildly romantic bitch/witch

let her simmer

sprinkle in bits of an incomprehensible
dabbler

bring to a boil

add previously sautéed chunks of five
old bald wrinkled academics

burn and feed to birds
you want to kill

Four Poems by Igor X

1.

Across the wide fishy sea a low cloud
hangs/a dusty drape/a languid mirror.

Your face in a cloud as dark as
your eyes.

Why have I come here? What dream
has filled my shoes with stones?

The sun suddenly collapses at my feet.
I pick it up. It's a rusty soda
bottle cap. I might have cut my foot/
bled spectacular sunsets onto the steppes.

Instead, I sneeze, toss the sun
into a child's discarded and broken
plastic bucket, sneeze again, creep home,
salute my forlorn bed, sink deep into a
warm depression.

2.

Oh great sky-scraping forests of mother
Russia! Do I slink among your muscular
trunks like a weasel? Or do I stand tall
to scrape the sky along with you?

That is the supreme, the ridiculous, the
unanswerable question I ask myself
as I fall out of bed on a freezing
Moscow morning, the interrogatory
that keeps repeating itself as I wait
for my borscht to cool.

3.

A newspaper crawls and scratches across Red Square
like a whining dog. No, I am wrong.
It is a whining dog that looks exactly like a newspaper.
The wind bites with hungry teeth, leaves a hole
bigger than a fist under my ribs.

Once again, I am foolishly roaming around
at 3 a.m. alone in the dark
waiting for something miraculous to happen,
a sign from the gods, a rain of sweet pickles
or the unprecedented arrival of thirteen rainbow-plumed
tropical birds/anything to break these cold unsmiling
stones.

Perhaps the whining newspaper/dog was a sign?
If so, as I now suspect, I completely missed
its significance. I usually do. I tend not to see
portents in things, especially when they are bursting
with them. I'd rather sit on them or throw them or
just eat them with pumpernickel.

I detest this labyrinth that crushes me
with concrete jaws, squeezes
until there is nothing for me to do
but slip out into the pit of night
seeking edible fungi in cemeteries.

4.

I remember as a boy fishing through Volga ice.
Where exactly, the precise spot, who knows?
All ice looks alike to me as do all frozen
rivers and all fish and all fishermen too
for that matter. Yes, and all people who
eat fish, especially while they are eating it.
All life blends into one grayish-white
fishpaste of a gelid field under which grass and
flowers and lovers scream for release. I
am such a flower, screaming so loudly the paper I
scream onto keeps disintegrating/melting ice/
cracking stones.

Am I a fish wanting to be caught by a poet
or a policeman? It doesn't matter, not
when all flowers become fish, and, as has happened
lately, all poets become policemen.

ESP

countergirl's no girl, 30ish,
zaftig, pretty, but always frowning;
the older raucous redhead
kiddingly complains that pretty
reads her mind. Pretty admits
she has that knack, so do her kids.

A countergirl with esp; if she
could read my mind
she'd throw me out.

The Process (2)

Ubiquitous stew of words to dip into
expectantly; the world lurching at me
chaotically;   aiming to avoid
calling things by their usual names
I risk misunderstanding.

No escape, I must call the sea
sea, the sky, sky, and all the rest,
with colors, shapes, conditions, textures
to reflect my mental weathers.
To skirt utter obscurity

I let this stand for that and such and such
mean so and so; dark and light, loud and
soft, cold and hot, dull and bright, all
opposition a music of nuance along a
private spectrum made public by my art.

Yet I hesitate in my translation
from world to word and back; what means
"burnt moons" or "stung blossoms"
to one not there when
the world punched those phrases from me?

Am I even partly comprehended?
Is all communication crippled? Sometimes
I don't understand myself. I'm not the same
man who now plunked down at desk typing
was last week smacked by a full-lipped sun.

Yet I write as if I were still there
tonguing that deep pink sky, as if memory
were infallible, as if you my listener
had taken a similar sun into your mouth and
sucked it fiery down.

I assault you with wild phrases,
shatter language into sweets and
toss the pieces at you. Care to play?
To catch and taste and know? Listen,
then call me poet?

OLD MAN

By what clever dodges has that old geezer
skulked into handsome and healthy
old age? By what subterfuges, cowardice,
cop outs, avoidances, lies? That tanned and
hearty old fucker! He looks so comfortable,
happy, self-satisfied, calm. He'll no doubt
die smiling in his sleep, painlessly,
surrounded by beautiful, sincerely weeping
loved ones, dozens of 'em.

What a rat, what a trickster, what a supremely
lucky bastard, to have survived so long and
well and to look so goddamn cocky about it.

EYAK

from The Guinness Book of World Records, *1977*

There are believed to be
20 or more
languages
including 6
North American Indian
languages
in which no one
can converse
because there is
only one speaker
left alive.

Eyak
is still spoken
in Southeast Alaska
by two aged sisters
when they meet.

EYAK (2)

Her sister dead,
the only human
she could talk to,
the ancient Eskimo
plods through snow
mumbling Eyak
to the winds.

Rosetta Speaks

The caped stranger escapes
into the ruined alphabet.
His rubbled past stares at him,
stony-eyed. Surprised
by familiar demons, their faces
his. The secret cat
sees everything.
Something wild and cellular
oozes out of a pyramid
to dominate texts. A fat
metaphysician turns pain
into pleasure. The mad poet
hacks away at logic, brains
splatter into melodies.
A cool Muse and a whistling mask
dream in maroon and purple.
The moon is bartered for pennies.
An elephant wanders through cities,
rewriting history.
Red blues rise where minarets and
spires stab exotic skies.
An abandoned dog, a black man
undoing his past, bits
of language drifting, smeared, chopped,
a dark crimson chorus, what
is known, made odd, not
really known at all, a riddle,
dangerous and beautiful, like
my woman.

GRIFFITH PARK

working here because I have to,
raking leaves, dumping garbage
meet a starving coyote whose glazed stare
reminds me of myself, seeking
meanings, truths, soul food,
among fallen twigs, each one
a lost and dried up life . . .

I hate the freezing 5 a.m. wakeups
to be in the park before seven, but I love
the slow subtle dawns over the hills,
the delicate leak of light that transmutes
the shapes and colors of trees,
the smells and sounds of woods,
the squirrels and birds, the raw
palpability of a great city park
just before daybreak, a giant brain asleep
before mind wakes, all the little noises
weaving this net of potential . . .

so I go about my business,
hefting stinking metal cans,
mucking and lurching through mudmaking
rains, as near earth as I'll ever get,
until that ineluctable end . . .

GRIFFITH PARK (2)

I'm told by an old Black Muslim
who's worked here for eons
that they daily find corpses
hastily buried in the woods,
never reported, no one knows
who they are, anonymous, and
anonymous they remain, someone's
runaway child, some drug deal
gone wrong, someone who said or
did the wrong thing to the wrong
person(s) at the wrong time,
derelicts and gays, husbands,
wives, boyfriends, girlfriends,
all sizes, shapes, ages and colors,
all one here, unknown, in this leafy
graveyard of the lost and
never found.

The Process (9)

The Truth's as elusive as the wrong
house on party night jumping from
street to street behind dark trees
to avoid our eyes.

The Truth slips among elaborate
metaphors like a quick seaspider down
glistening crevices. There are no hands
nimble enough to pluck it from its
jewelbox.

The Truth's an intricate jumble
of innumerable filaments
each untouchable, yet
in the graceful motion of a skilled
shuttler, a dance to another space.

Truths captured in jars of words
are dead scales scraped from
once swift fish; think of
tiger's leap, tales of light,
music slipping simile's traps,
the luscious yang of now.

Truth's too rich for our feeble senses;
we hear echoes and vibrations only,
barely glimpse what's given.

Unwrap eyes, reverse skins...
feel the beat of a world
begging to be known.

A Disappeared Poet

He faded into shredded billboards, burnt bedding,
sunset shade
he slipped between layers of slate
his seafingers harp the piers
he is everywhere

He puzzles through vaults
he runs with hounds
he is among the skimmers and the plums
he is everywhere

When a treehead vibrates with evening gossip crows,
he sings
he has vanished into things unseen, but
he is everywhere

WAITING

one day you'll say it
the line rippling out like a purple wave
from the long-playing sea,
something terrible and strange

it could slit open the world, such a line
make rocks weep a long-sought answer or
an unheard-of question, it could
shock crowds to their feet
cheering and shouting, begging for more

it could be the truest thing
you ever said, as true and obvious as
your mouth

so you go after it, mumbling, typing, talking
to yourself (people stare, shake their heads)
and you get parts of it, maybe, like flecks of
dawn at the edge of a wing

but it's never quite the thing you know
must be there
the pearl, the flower, the moment
when notes flow so easily
you wonder why you haven't
heard them before

and you chase it, keep chasing it, a mad
lepidopterist
juggling sounds and words, images and breaths
certain it's there, fanatic in your faith

and maybe you've glimpsed it
as it brushed you, begging for light,
some mumbled magic, a brilliant accident, even

and maybe it's revealed itself
in half-remembered reveries
or conceals itself in overheard conversations,
traffic backfires and dusk-flooded alleys

or maybe you still haven't got it
because you don't know what it is
and you've never known what it is
wouldn't know it if it perched
like a pixie right on your nose

though there's ample evidence
that it happens, occasionally, so
you keep gambling it'll happen again,
opening yourself to everything, trusting

Poem From A Line By Olson

from the union
of mind and ear
the syllable is born
as from the you and
the me
the us and the child

from far and close
the center found
the synthesis
discovered
from union
not merely juxtaposing
but union
the coming together

overlapping and loving
of sense in all senses
this music
arises
as a diphthong
of forces
a pearl of frictions
an inevitable rhythm
of incoming probings

lovely opposings
so sweet in their
discords
so measured
in their shiftings

as water and rock
make stone mana round
smooth as melted-down
moon in the palm

truer than moon
because mine

This River

when I write about the world
do I disturb it
as a rock disturbs a pool

do I draw off anything from it
by speaking of it
as if drawing water from a pool

or do I absorb its spirit
into the poem, as the spirit of water
enters a poem about water, making it flow

The Process (4)

I get none of it right. I don't even know
who you are.

The closer I peer the stranger IT
becomes. One world disappears
into another, rules reverse,
inhabitants grow limbs and eyes, their
babble indecipherable, movements
random, poetry unknowable.

Words, where do you aim? At
Platoed furniture which
disintegrates upon clumsily carried out
inspection? Words,
fictions, self-referring entities, a closed
universe of paragraphs, a mesh of lies.

There's nothing nameable out there,
(names being arbitrary, virtual jokes)
there's nothing graspable out there
(phenomena fall apart when too closely observed)
there's only whatever's out there
out there.

And we, pontificating at each other
of truth and reality
and the world words mean . . .

Where in the void are we
and what in hell are we gibbering about?

CREMATION

an efficient disappearing act

but now even your bones
are nothing, ashes
sprinkled on waves, waves
rolling away and away, back
and back

so, no special place for us
to cry or place a stone or
flowers, no plaque or marker
to clean carefully, reverently,
no spot that is yours . . .

except the ocean, its roar,
its tears, ours
its body, yours

and when I swim, now,
I am with you again,
your sweat, the ocean
your laughter, the waves,
as I was with you as a child,
wrestling in bed or on the beach,

I am with you again.

Urgent Message

On April First, I
madly plan, as if immortal,
innumerable projects—how many
heartbeats left? Eternity's
a laughing mouth, a cave
with teeth of flame, and I
leap in, crazy poet, crazy
painter, crazy to get things
done, made, now
before the tick-tock of
darkness; the sun burns a hole
in my heart, eyes
full moons, mind fixed on
one deep purple idea:
finish things fast,
do them well but finish them,
now, before the body becomes
shadow, before mind leaks out
through nostrils and disappears
into mist, before there's
nothing left of me but
a scribble on a rock . . .

News

Red/yellow/purple petals
headline the grass.

Several witty columns tossed off
by trees.

Weather reports itself smogless
after morning haze retreats.

Sports section: ants and flies
vie for first.

Obituaries: many dried up worms, dead dog
on the freeway, a few smashed possums and
a dilatory pigeon.

Forecast: more browned leaves, buckled sidewalks,
unexplained thumpings under the roof.

Fire in the hills, flu bug
in the air vents.

Tufts of life cling to brick,
all the little dyings
bathed in light.

Business report: erratic fluctuations
in the market for dreams.

The eternal, slow motion flux
and reflux of things.

I breathe, I see, I stumble between lines.
I'm still part of what's happening.

PRAYER

for Murray Wolfe

In spun light
I'm woven
a tapestried
animal/knight
in trousers
drawn toward dinner
under an arch of palms

Perverfid blossoms!
Each moment's petal
a heart-piercing flash!   Alive
and dying, dying yet alive!
Flesh of sky
throbbing, sensing.   Eyes
gemmed with tears.

Forgive me, gods,
for omissions and
bumblings; forgive me, Sweet
Self, for all
I did not see
and therefore failed
to love.

A LITTLE NIGHT JAZZ

```
                              t        d
                    c         t     e
twilight pigeons              a     r
              s               e
```

along phone lines/melody
I begin to parse/but
one pigeon takes off/changing
the tune

begin again

another moves a bit/the song
changes

I could keep this up for hours
until all the music

flies away

ABOUT THE AUTHOR:

Originally from Brooklyn, New York, he moved to Southern California in 1978. He has been drawing and painting since childhood, but began writing in his mid-thirties. He hosted *The Poetry Connexion* on Pacifica radio from October 1981 though early 1996. He has worked for Amnesty International, PEN's Freedom to Write Committee, and on many local Los Angeles and California issues. A teacher of art, English and literature, poetry and philosophy, he is also an accomplished painter. His artwork is in several private and academic collections including the Ruth & Marvin Sackner Archive of Concrete and Visual Poetry, Mills College, Berkeley, the Athenaeum in La Jolla, California, and Otis College of Art and Design in Los Angeles. His complex "specialties" are one-of-a-kind books (one from which the cover of this book was taken) filled with paintings and collages, some made using a burn technique, and/or combining poetry and graphics to create an array of spectacular effects (abstracts, figures, landscapes and "unknown languages"). His honors include the one man show "Austin Straus—Collages: Word + Image," an exhibition (and poetry reading), February and March 2000 at Beyond Baroque Gallery, Venice, California. He was a 1997-98 "Writers on Site" resident, sponsored by the Los Angeles County Museum of Art (LACMA) and Beyond Baroque Literary/Arts Center. He currently resides in Southern California with his wife of 28 years, poet and writer Wanda Coleman. *Intensifications* is his second book of poems.